MILKSHAKE

Favourite Foods

Birthday Cake
Chips
Chocolate
Ice-Cream
Milkshake
Pizza

All words that appear in **bold** are explained in the glossary on page 30

First published in 1993 by
Wayland (Publishers) Ltd
61 Western Road, Hove
East Sussex BN3 1JD, England
© Copyright 1993 Wayland (Publishers) Ltd

Editor: Francesca Motisi
Research: Anne Moses

British Library Cataloguing in Publication Data
Moses, Brian
    Milkshake.—(Favourite Foods Series)
    I. Title   II. Gordon, Mike   III. Series
    664

    ISBN 0-7502-0634-9

Typeset by Dorchester Typesetting Group Ltd
Printed and bound in Belgium by Casterman, S.A.

MILKSHAKE

Written by Brian Moses

Illustrated by Mike Gordon

Wayland

You can
drink your
milkshake
alone,

or with a friend,

while
watching
television,

or at a party.

One way to make a milkshake is by whisking a spoonful of powdered milkshake with milk in a bowl, or using a **blender**.

Powdered milkshakes are made in factories. They usually include sugar, dried **glucose** syrup, **flavouring** and natural colours.

These **ingredients** are mixed together and passed through two machines which turn the mixture into powder.

Next the powder is packed into special boxes. These keep it fresh while it is waiting to be sold in shops and supermarkets.

You can make a
milkshake with real fruit,
instead of using the
instant powder.

To do this you will need
milk, fruit and ice-cream.

Ask an adult to
help you liquidize
a banana or some
strawberries.

Then whisk this up with milk and ice-cream, or mix it in a tall glass using a long spoon.

Where do you think all the ingredients for our milkshake come from?

Most of the milk comes from cows.
Cows are milked early in the
morning and in the evening.

They used to be milked by hand but farmers now use electric milking machines.

The milk is stored in tanks where it is cooled. It is then collected by **tankers** and driven to the dairy.

At the dairy the milk is heated up to kill any **germs**. This is called **pasteurisation**.

Then the milk bottles and cartons move along a **conveyor belt** to a filling machine. The milk is delivered in cartons to supermarkets.

Milk is also an ingredient in
ice-cream and this is often used
in recipes for milkshakes.

To make milkshakes taste nice we need to add different flavours.

Some milkshakes are flavoured with chocolate or toffee.

Others are flavoured with fruits, such as raspberry and blackcurrant. These fruits come from many different places.

Some of the fruit is grown in other countries.

Bananas and pineapples come from hot **tropical** countries ...

like Africa or the West Indies.

Kiwi fruit comes from New Zealand

and mangoes from the West Indies,

but strawberries are grown all over the world.

Here are some ideas for milkshakes that you might like to try making yourself. All of the amounts are for one person.

Either mix in a blender (ask an adult to help you with this), or whisk in a tall jug with a hand whisk.

CARAMEL CRACKER

You will need:

150 ml fresh milk (5 fl oz or $\frac{1}{4}$ pint)
A good squeeze of caramel dessert sauce
1 heaped tablespoon of vanilla ice-cream

Whisk and pour mixture into
a glass. Top with a little
grated chocolate.

RASPBERRY RAZZLE

You will need:

150 ml fresh milk (5 fl oz or $1/4$ pint)
2 heaped tablespoons tinned raspberries
(in fruit juice)
A heaped tablespoon of raspberry-ripple
ice-cream
1 teaspoon of runny honey

Mix and pour into a glass. Top with a little whipped cream and three or four whole raspberries.

BLACKCURRANT RECORD-BREAKER

You will need:

150 ml fresh milk (5 fl oz or $\frac{1}{4}$ pint)
1 dessertspoon of pure blackcurrant cordial
(or blackcurrant and apple)
2 tablespoons of blackcurrant yoghurt.

Blend or whisk together and top with whipped cream.

Make your own milkshakes using different fruits, flavourings and decorations.

Frosted Glasses

Put some caster sugar in a saucer, or shallow bowl. ⇨

Use half a lemon and ⇦ rub this round the top of the glass.

Then dip the glass in the sugar and the top ⇨ will look frosty.

The Perfect Milkshake

Banana with grated chocolate,
kiwi fruit or pear,
If I made the perfect milkshake
I wouldn't be stopping there . . .

I'd add strawberries and melon,
pineapple and toffee,
mix it up with hazelnuts
and a tablespoon of coffee,

all topped with a glacé cherry
and a double squirt of cream,
the taste would be quite heavenly,
just like drinking a dream!

Glossary

Blender   An electric machine that mixes foods together.

Conveyor Belt   A moving belt that moves things from one place to another.

Flavouring   Something added to food or drink to give it a particular taste.

Germs   Things that are alive but too small to see. Some can make people ill.

Glucose   A kind of sugar.

Ingredients   Ingredients are all separate things you need for making something, a cake, for example.

Pasteurisation   The milk is heated to kill any germs.

Tankers   Large trucks that carry liquids, such as milk.

Temperature   How hot or cold something is.

Tropical   Belonging to areas of the world where there is great heat and heavy rainfall.

Acknowledgements
The author and publisher would like to thank the National Dairy Council and Nestlé UK Ltd for their advice.

Notes for parents and teachers

Read the book with children, either individually or in groups. Talk about the illustrations as you turn each page. Ask children for their favourite flavours. In the classroom a simple chart could be produced showing favourite flavours and questions written to go with it – which flavour is liked the most? Which is liked least? Do more boys than girls like one particular kind? Do adults enjoy drinking milkshakes? Children could question their families.

Have children seen cows being milked? Perhaps a trip could be arranged to a farm so that children could watch what happens. A simple flow chart could be produced showing what happens to the milk after it leaves the cow. Older children should be able to talk about the process and to remember the order in which things happen.

Find out about other foods that are made from milk – cream, butter, cheese, yoghurt. Milkshake is a milk based drink, what other drinks have milk added to them?

What can children find out about Louis Pasteur and his discovery? Can they also find out why milk is such a healthy food?

Part of the classroom might become a Milk Bar. Children could write menus on milkshake-shaped card. The various items could be priced and children invited to add up different orders.

On a large map of the world, mark in the different countries where fruit that is used to flavour milkshake is grown. Which of these are hot tropical countries?

Read the poem *The Perfect Milkshake* and ask children to list the ingredients that they would include. This could then be drawn, or designed as a collage. Perhaps it could even be made up into a drink! Does it taste perfect? What would it be called? Suggest that children advertise their drink in a way that might make others keen to try it. Can they think of an eye-catching slogan?

Children who make up the recipes for milkshakes will discover how food changes when it is blended or whisked.

The above suggestions will satisfy a number of statements of attainment in National Curriculum guidelines for English, Maths and Science at Key Stage 1.

Books to read

A Picnic of Poetry – Poems about food and drink, selected by Anne Harvey (Blackie 1988/Puffin 1990) contains 'Chocolate Milk'.

Thawing Frozen Frogs by Brian Patten (Viking 1990/ Puffin 1992) includes a poem 'The Milk-shake Cafe'

Milk by Dorothy Turner (Wayland, 1988)

Milk by Catherine de Sairigne (Moonlight Publishing Ltd; 1987)

Michael the Milk Bottle, **Up From the Country**, **On Your Doorstep**, **Good Things to Eat** Four booklets available free of charge from the National Dairy Council, 5-7 John Princes Street, London W1M OAP.

Index